R

THE
CREATIVE EDGE

Fostering Innovation
Where You Work

WILLIAM C. MILLER

PERSEUS PUBLISHING

Cambridge, Massachusetts

Many of the designations used by manufacturers and sellers to dis-
tinguish their products are claimed as trademarks. Where those
designations appear in this book and Perseus Books was aware of
a trademark claim, the designations have been printed in initial
caps (e.g. MacPaint) or all caps (e.g. SABRE).

Library of Congress Cataloging-in-Publication Data

Miller, William C. (William Cox), 1948–
    The creative edge.

    Includes index.
    1. Creative ability in business.   I. Title.
HD53.M55   1986   650.1   86-14097
ISBN 0-201-15045-X
ISBN 0-201-52401-5 (pbk.)

Perseus Publishing books are available at special discounts for bulk purchases
in the U.S. by corporations, institutions, and other organizations. For more
information ,please contact the special Markets department at the Perseus
Books Group, 11 Cambridge Center, Cambridge, MA 02142 or call (617)252-5298

Cover Design by Steve Snider
Text design by Laura Fredericks
Set in 10 point Palatino by Compset, Inc. Beverly, MA

Perseus Books is a member of the Perseus Books Group
3 4 5 6 7 8 9 10

www.perseuspublishing.com